P E R U

AN ANCIENT ANDEAN CIVILIZATION

WHITE STAR PUBLISHERS

Text
Mario Polia

Contents

1 *The profile of this Sicuani native is a symbol of modern-day Peru. Both Indian and Spanish blood run through his veins, but the ancient pride of his ancestors shines through. The typical Andean hat, known as the chullo, was the origin of the name cholo, which now means mestizo.*

2-3 *Reflecting the last light of day, the peaks of Chopicalqui (21,000 feet) in the Cordillera Blanca stand out against the impending mystery of the Andean night. Offerings are still made to these mountains, the home of the protective gods known as the apus and the setting of ancestral myths.*

4-5 *The lazy winding of the Amazon River near Iquitos is like a snake moving slowly through the green vegetation. The yakumama, the maternal spirit of the water, takes the form of a gigantic anaconda that hides in riverbeds, according to native myths.*

6-7 *Misti Volcano, 17,340 feet high, is surrounded by a lunar landscape of ash and lava, while elegant vicuñas (Lama vicugna) graze among sparse tufts of ichu, a high-altitude grass plant.*

8 *The icy waters of the Andean plateau, at an elevation of about 13,000 feet, reflect the eternal glaciers of the Cordillera Blanca.*

9 *A reed (totora) boat, whose form has remained unchanged over the centuries, plies the tranquil waters of Lake Titicaca. According to native traditions, this is where the present world was created and the sun, moon, and stars first emerged.*

10-11 *This aerial view of Lima shows the church of the Sagrado Corazón de María, the Avenida Independencia, and the populous Magdalena del Mar district. The Peruvian people are very religious, and great churches contrast with modest homes.*

© 2003, 2006 White Star S.p.A.
Via C. Sassone, 22/24
13100 Vercelli, Italy
www.whitestar.it

Translation
A.B.A. MILAN

ISBN 978-88-544-0135-8

REPRINTS:
3 4 5 6   14 13 12 11 10

Printed in China
Color separation: Chiaroscuro, Turin

Introduction

Peru is a geographical anachronism and a melting pot of cultures. In an area five times as large as Italy but with half its population, different cultures with different roots and languages coexist, united by a strong feeling of belonging to the same fatherland. The term "Indian," which lost its racial meaning long ago, still retains its cultural significance; the heritage of the pre-Colombian cultures lives on in the Indian's view of the world, social structures, religion, and art. If speakers of the Andean languages and the various languages of the Selva are combined into one group, only a relative minority speaks Spanish. Leaving the big cities and venturing into the Andes or the Selva, it is essential to remember this fact in order to understand Peru and enjoy the unique charm of a country with a glorious history, in which ancient and modern coexist and interact.

Some very different geographical features and ecosystems also coexist in Peru. These include the coastal deserts, which are among the most arid in the world, such as the Sechura Desert in the north; the hot, sunny regions of the lower Western slopes of the Andes; the temperate climate of the Andean area between 6,000 and 11,500 feet above sea level, the land of maize and agriculture; the cold climate of the jalca, the land of edible tubers, as high as 13,000 feet, and the even colder puna, up to nearly 16,000 feet; and the polar climate of the highest part of the Andes, with its permanent glaciers and snowfields.

Descending the Andean spurs, eroded by rushing torrents, to the east, we enter the high, rainy Selva, and lower down, at around 3,000 feet above sea level, the rainforest, with its placid, majestic rivers and tall trees, the land of the last indigenous tribes, the jaguar, the cayman, and the great snakes.

Lima, the modern heart of Peru, has to be the first stop on our journey, not only because the plane lands there, but also for its magnificent museums and monuments. The city, which spends three months of the year under a pale sun, three more under a bright sun, and six shrouded in a damp fog, is also a land of contrasts. Alongside its ultra-modern skyscrapers, grand hotels, and desperately poor areas that surround the city in a vice-like grip stand colonial mansions with spacious patios and ancient pyramids between modern buildings or on the edge of busy streets. All this is accompanied by the smell of the sea, the fragrance of tropical flowers, and the sweet smell of air pollution as mini-skirted girls mingle with the solemn women of the sierra with their inscrutable expressions and tall hats selling herbs and talismans by the roadside in the town center.

After Lima, the next stop is Cuzco, which can be reached by road or air. Visitors who fly into Cuzco are liable to suffer from soroche (mountain sickness), while

those who travel by road suffer the discomfort of the long walk. In either case, it is a fair price to pay to see one of the most amazing places in the world.

You cannot know Peru if you have never been to Cuzco, capital of the Inca empire and sacred center of the Andean world for over 500 years, until the Spanish conquest, after which it was a point of conflict and union between two worlds.

Visitors to Cuzco need a few days to adjust to the climate, enjoy its beauty, and admire the sights of the surrounding area, such as Sacsayhuamán, the fortified temple that overlooks the town, built from blocks whose perfect fit and size defy time and reason: some are as tall as a two-story building. Sacsayhuamán, whose gigantic walls imitate the shape of lightning, should be visited immediately, either early in the morning or at sunset, when the sun flows like liquid gold down the stairways and through the majestic doors. It is a pilgrimage to one of the most impressive monuments ever built by man.

There are, of course, other sights to see. Kenko is marked by sacred monoliths and carved rocks over which rainwater flowed during rites celebrated at planting time. Pucapucara (the Red Fortress) is located near Tambomachay, where water gushes from squared stone fountains at the foot of elegant walls. Ollantaytambo, with its impressive terraces and long stairways, boasts a huge fortress and the temple sacred to Inti (the Sun), which housed the entrails of dead kings whose mummies lay in the Sun Temple at Cuzco. Finally, in Pusac, with its magnificent ruins and the market with its many colors and scents, native women wearing brightly colored skirts and long braids sit on the ground, keeping guard over their potatoes and vegetables and suspiciously staring through slit eyes at the intrusive tourists who photograph everything and buy nothing but trinkets and fake flutes.

Then, early in the morning, we board the little train for Machu Picchu, a faraway dream of sun and stone. Perched on rocks that slope sheer down to the rushing Urubamba River, this was the secret place where, as the Inca empire fell to the Spanish harquebuses, the last Sun Virgins were hidden in order to perform a vital task: to pray to the gods for victory. They carried out this task until they died of old age, and their corroded bones were found by archaeologists, together with their liturgical instruments. A handful of warriors and faithful servants tilled the terraces and defended the entrances, but it was all in vain. Even though the Spaniards never discovered the existence of that sacred outpost, the Andean gods seemed to have signed an armistice with the God who came from over the seas.

On returning to Cuzco, visitors can lose themselves in its ancient streets with their squared stone Inca walls, visit the colonial mansions and churches built with stone from kings' palaces, stroll under the porticoes of Plaza de Armas, and listen to the great cathedral bell, made of bronze mixed with Inca gold.

After Cuzco, amid green plateaus and lowering skies, comes Titicaca, or "wildcat rock lake" (titi means both wildcat and rock). Legend has it that the Incas saw a feline with eyes of flame on the dark rocks, which was believed to be the spirit of the place. Lake Titicaca, at an altitude of 12,500 feet, is a sea that changes color according to the

12 top *On the buttresses of Pisaq, or "Partridge Mountain," the Incas built a temple dedicated to the cult of Inti, the Sun, their mythical father.*

12 bottom *The ramparts of the fortified temple of Saqsayhuamán, in the province of Cuzco, defy time and logic. It is natural to wonder how its builders transported the enormous rocks used to make its walls, and how they were worked to fit together perfectly in a complex, three-dimensional pattern of insets.*

13 *The western side of Machu Picchu: from the temple with its seven niches dedicated the Andean creator Wiraqucha, a little stairway leads to the Intiwatana terrace. This is the site of astronomical observations and ritual worship of the sun on the solstice (Inti Raymi). In the background stands mighty Wayna Picchu.*

time of day and the climate. When the sky is clear, it is cobalt colored, and the clouds are reflected so perfectly in it that you feel dizzy, as if the world had suddenly turned upside down.

Boats with tall curved prows rowed by silent fishermen glide over the calm waters. These boats, made from totora (reeds with edible shoots that grow plentifully on the shores of the lake) are identical to the ones used by the Uru, Lupaca, and other ancient peoples. Artificial totora islands are anchored to the bottom of the lake, becoming soft areas gilded by yellow fishermen's huts. There are some particularly sacred islands, containing the ruins of ancient temples and convents of the virgins dedicated to the cult, destroyed by time and the Jesuits, such as the islands of the Sun and Moon, which mark the spot from where the stars rose.

The Aymara people, like the Incas, consider Lake Titicaca the navel of the world. It is not just a lake: it is the sacred birthplace of the people of the Andes. The legends that the Spaniards wrote down in the mid-sixteenth century still live on in the hearts of the taciturn highland shepherds. They tell them to their children at night, sitting round a smoky fire fuelled by cattle and llama dung, while the icy wind of the puna shrieks and shakes the mud and stone huts scattered over the steppes.

They tell of Viracocha, a bearded white man, who lay hidden in the dark waters of the lake before this world existed. At the dawn of time, when the earth was still shrouded in darkness, Viracocha decided to make creatures to worship him. He created the first human beings at Tiahuanaco (now in Bolivia), but he soon tired of those gigantic men, with their fearful strength and hearts as dark as the shadows they lived in. They neither worshipped him nor obeyed the laws he gave them: impiety, war, and black magic were their only laws. Consequently, he brought forth the sun, moon, and stars from the waters, and made fire rain down on the world. Then he opened the cataracts of the new sky and flooded the land. The giants either drowned or burned to death. Some turned into blackish rocks scattered over the steppes and others into the mute stone giants that still stand in Tiahuanaco.

However, some of them guessed the god's intentions and hid in deep underground caves where light and heat could not reach them. On moonless nights they roam the steppe in human form. They teach the laika (witchdoctors) in dreams, giving them the power to spread evil and kill by magic. Now, there are many laika mingling with the farmers and shepherds. No one knows who they are, but everyone fears them, as a dark, looming menace. On the last day of the world, when the sun goes out, the giants will come back to earth and devour the surviving men.

After the era of the giants, the first Incas, sons of the Sun, emerged from the sacred caves of Cuzco and founded a new world where justice reigned. They divided it into four parts and placed at its center Cuzco, or pachap-sunqu: the sacred heart of the world. They destroyed hunger with the power of work and the gift of mother earth, the same color as gold but even more precious, maize. They built magnificent cities and fortresses, irrigated the fields, traced paths that the people of the Andes still use today, and threw daring suspension bridges across the mountain gorges. They tamed the mountains by terracing their slopes and

filling them with fertile soil. Visitors traveling through the narrow valleys crossed by impetuous rivers, on their way to Pisac or Ollantaytambo, can still admire the andenes, the ancient terraces where maize is still grown today.

The era of the Incas ended on the day established by the gods with the arrival of the viracocha, the white men, who conquered the world created by the god who had emerged from the lake. They taught the Indians to call him by a new name and worship him with new rites. The Sun of the Incas was extinguished, and a multitude of Indians died in the mines of Laicacota or in the bowels of the cerro rico in Potosì to supply silver to the Spanish crown. Others fled to the edge of the snowfields and to ever more desolate places, where they died of hunger, longing, and heartbreak.

The old men tell stories in the Aymara language, while the women poke the fire, squatting on the ground. A hen sits on her eggs in a dark corner. Children and grandchildren listen, receiving the precious gift of tradition, without which their bronze skin and almond eyes would be no more than exotic attributes for tourists and their video cameras. One day they will work as shepherds, and some of them may go to university, but most of them will never forget those tales and will hand down their living memory to the generation of the third millennium.

The ancestral spirits, called achachila (grandparents), keep watch on the highest mountains – the Illampu, Illimani, and Sajama – receiving from their descendants offerings of coca and tobacco leaves, llama fetuses, sweets, and alcohol in exchange for the gift of rain, fertility of animals and women, protection of the fields against hail, snow, and frost, and protection of their homes against

14 *On the floating islands of Lake Titicaca, a descendant of the Uru prepares bundles of* totora, *the reed used to build boats and houses. Its seedlings offer an iodine-rich food.*

15 *Among the last few spurs of the Andes, Lake Titicaca can be seen from the road to Puno.*

lightning. On Christmas Eve, a llama is killed, and its blood is sprinkled on the potato fields. The same offerings are buried for Mother Earth to eat. Every community has its own achachila and a patron saint; the concept of "society" is unconceivable without the worship of common ancestors and a saint, without a sacred base.

In fields surrounded by eucalyptus trees, where corn, barley, oats, and quinua, with its tiny grains full of nutritional virtues, are grown, ancient rites are performed. Not far away, the electric lights of Puno are reflected in the lake, and the headlights of trucks illuminate the highland night. There are doctors and health centers here and there, but native specialists in traditional medicine are perhaps even more numerous. The akulliri diagnoses diseases according to the flavor of coca. The jampiri knows the secrets of herbs and magic spells, whereas the ajayiru calls back souls which have fled from their bodies after a fright or been abducted by evil spirits. The anchanchu live in deserted spots and take on the shape of dwarves, while women kidnapped by the dead watch over the chullpa (ancient funeral towers) at Sillustani on the lakeshore.

Ancient and modern coexist like European and Indian blood in the veins of the Aymara, like the sacred waters of the lake and the motor boats, the totora islands where the Uru lived and the asphalted roads, and the achachila and the airplanes that disappear beyond the puna in a sky whose deep blue remains engraved on the soul forever.

This is Peru: a world where the past has never passed away and extends beyond the present, challenging the future. The train that speeds away to the west at times follows the ancient paths traveled by the highland shepherds to exchange the meager produce of their land – dried llama meat (charki), fine alpaca and vicuna wool, and dehydrated potatoes (chuño) – for maize and precious sea salt.

The best way of enjoying the Andean panorama is to travel to Puna by train from Cuzco and continue down by train to Arequipa, the white queen of the sierra. At an altitude of just over 7,500 feet, at the foot of the Chachani (19,935 feet) and Misti (19,145 feet) volcanoes with their permanent ice caps that are surprisingly reminiscent of Fujiyama, stands Arequipa (the white city). Amid green oases cultivated as orchards in a mild climate that produces several harvests a year, it offers lavishly decorated churches, shady streets, and cool colonial casonas (mansions) built with local stone, the white sillar.

In the town center there is a heart that no longer beats: the Convent of Santa Catalina. It should be visited leisurely as it will surely leave its mark on your soul. In the sixteenth and seventeenth centuries, a corner of Castille was reconstructed on over 65,000 feet of sacred land for the nuns who then thronged the cells with their flower-filled windows, cool, tidy cloisters, and paved paths. Many of the young daughters of wealthy Spanish families either joyfully spent their lives there as a vocation or watched their youth fade with resignation within the silent walls painted in red and yellow ochre dotted by austere, aristocratic widows, as they prayed, dreamt, and cultivated the language and literature of faraway Spain.

In the ancient convent, time has stood still. Everything is still in its place: red geraniums and roses bloom in the original vases, and water flows bubbling through the same clean channels as in bygone days. Every so often the wind blows open a worm-eaten door that creaks, and silent ghosts seem to glide through the cloisters.

Beyond the oases, volcanic and river activity has modeled the land, covering it with a thick coat of lava and ash, like a moonscape. The river Majes has excavated its bed, creating a 9,800-foot-deep canyon between the mighty peaks of the Coropuna (over 21,000 feet) and Ampato (over 20,600 feet) volcanoes.

The frozen body of a teenage girl was recently discovered amid the snow and ice of the Ampato Volcano. She had been dedicated by the Incas to the apu, the gods of the high peaks, so that they would grant the gift of water and placate the power of the fire that lies concealed in the heart of the mountains and rends the earth. She had been prepared for the sacrifice and to serve as a messenger. She was killed with a single skillful blow on the temple with a club. Her descendants renamed her Juanita, la dama de Ampato (Juanita, the lady of Ampato). She was buried in the glacier, curled up as if to protect herself against a fate too cruel for her tender years.

Human victims have not been sacrificed to the great mountains of ice and fire for a long time, but the apu live on in the hearts of the people of the sierra. They receive humbler offerings in honor of the same ancient faith; a faith that over 400 years of forced coexistence with white men, the terror of the Spanish corregidores, the zeal of missionaries, radio, roads, and compulsory schooling have not wiped out.

From Arequipa the road leads straight to the sea, and at lower altitudes steppes and dusty cactuses replace the trees. Then, the road runs along the sea to Lomas, 170 miles further north, crossing green valleys following the courses of rivers that interrupt the monotony of the deserts and flow

16 *In one of the porticoes of the Monastery of Santa Catalina of Arequipa, founded in 1580, the light of the tropics tinges the ancient plaster's whitewash a rosy hue.*

17 top *The* pileta, *the fountain in the Santa Catalina Monastery, has gurgled for four centuries. Red ochre,* white volcanic stone (sillar), *and a bright blue sky give this ancient monastery a distinctive, unforgettable charm.*

17 bottom *Plumes of smoke drift lazily from the top of Misti, but this drowsy giant often awakes, causing violent earthquakes that shake the city of Arequipa.*

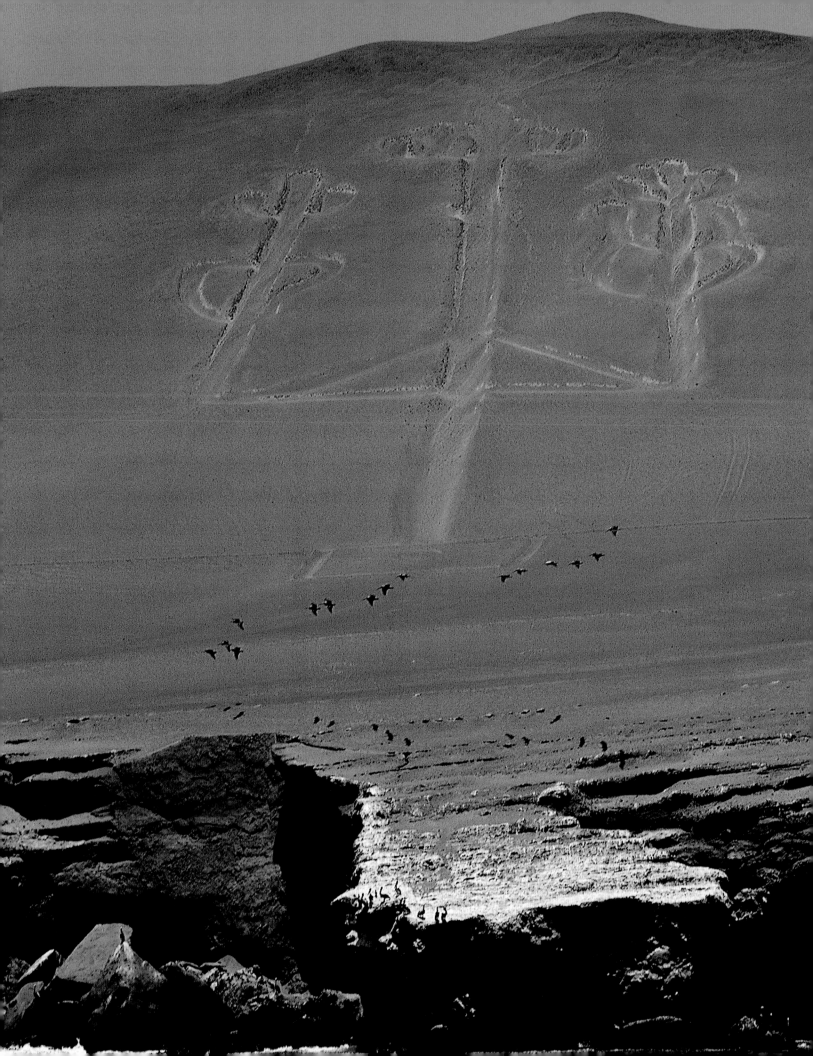

into the Pacific. Then it heads inland, to Nazca, famous for the mysterious signs traced in the desert that measure up to 980 feet long and portray birds with snake-like necks, hummingbirds, monkeys, lizards, spiders, and quadrupeds. These signs were made to be seen only from the sky, but by who, and why? Were they a silent payer to bring down the blessing of rain on a life that otherwise could not exist? Generations of researchers have been unable to solve the mystery.

About 60 miles further north lies Ica, in the green heart of an oasis crossed by the river of the same name and irrigated by cool channels, full of orchards and cotton plantations and above all vines transplanted by the first Spaniards, together with olives and sugar cane. The generous soil, warmed by the sun, produces good wines, the best in Peru, while the grape stalks are used to make pisco, one of the best-known liqueurs in the country, with its inimitable flavor of tropical sun and the fragrance of the wood used to make the barrels.

Here, there were once small, flourishing fiefdoms governed by local curacas, who later became vassals of the Incas. The Spaniards divided the land into huge estates called latifundios that took hours

to cross on horseback. There they founded their haciendas: fortified farms with whitewashed walls, a church, and the owner's residence, with its large inner courtyards and shady rooms, grain storehouses, workshops, dark cellars with wooden wine-presses, and stables.

These were small towns, tiny kingdoms whose subjects, until the 1960's when the latifundios were abolished by the Agricultural Reform, were ragged half-castes whose blood was largely Indian. They used to start work after the dawn mass and continue from sunrise to sunset under the pitiless sun and the equally pitiless gaze of the capataz (overseer). They grew used to suffering in silence like their companions in misfortune of the previous century, the African slaves, though the slaves vented their feelings at night with guitars, singing, and dancing. Those songs, with their tribal rhythms – cumbias, ciumananas, etc. – have become part of the present-day soul of Peru.

At Ica it is still possible to visit the old haciendas with their scent of cedar, tropical wood, and whitewash, their long colonnades and flower-filled patios, old carved furniture, long tables large enough to seat the patriarchal families of yesteryear, and oil paintings of ancestors who frown on the noisy tourists in the twilight.

A little to the north of Ica the cool enchantment of the oasis dissolves, and a desert of sunbaked sand dunes stretches as far as the eye can see. Here and there stand slender date palms imported from Africa, but instead of camels, small caravans of donkeys travel the dunes carrying food or water to and from goodness knows where.

Just before the town of Pisco, the squat desert peninsula of Paracas, named after the winds that blow there, stretches out into the Pacific. The subsoil of Paracas conceals the most attractive man-made fabrics of the Americas. Those fabrics shroud dried-up bodies some 2,500 years old, buried in deep tombs. The amazing colors of the great mantos (cloaks) housed in the museums of Lima and Ica seem to ignore the passing of time. Rows of absurd hybrids of human bodies with animals and plants, the gods of a forgotten mythology, are woven into the fabrics. There are numerous figures of felines and snakes, images of the power of water and the subsoil. They hold fruit, pods, and plants in their claws, and sometimes cut-off heads, perhaps those of the spirits of famine and drought, or human victims sacrificed in exchange for water, more precious than gold. Herds of seals and sea lions lie lazily in the sun among the rocks on the beach, which have been eroded into weird shapes by the wind, sun, and salt over the millennia.

18 *The Paracas "candelabra," once attributed to the ancients, may only be a gigantic signpost left over from the wars for Peruvian independence, indicating the position of the port from a distance.*

19 top *Colonies of sea lions populate the rocky beaches of the coast of Paracas and the Ballestas islands.*

19 bottom *Pacific waves crash along the coast of Sechura in northern Peru.*

From Pisco a road winds up through the spurs of the Andes, along the edge of precipices, leading to Huancavelica, Ayacucho, Abancay, and Cuzco – another road to travel, and another adventure to experience. Huancavelica, situated at an altitude of over 11,800 feet, is a name that evokes the idea of hell in the memory of the natives. For four centuries, thousands uprooted from their land died slowly, crushed by fatigue and poisoned by the mercury of the mines. They attributed their death to the wrath and curse of Amaru, the great snake, spirit-guardian of the treasures of the earth whose kingdom they had been forced to defile by the insatiable greed of the white men.

Huancavelica, surrounded by high peaks, is a land of witchdoctors (danzaq) who perform the danza de las tijeras, named after the two tinkling scissor-shaped blades with which they accompany their frenetic steps and incredible contortions for hours, until they reach ecstasy. The stamping of their feet awakens Mother Earth, who makes the maize seeds turgid, the pastures green, and the waters that flow down from the mountains copious. The people believe that the wamani, the spirit of the mountains in the shape of a great invisible falcon, grasps the danzaq with its claws and flies upwards with him, making him perform amazing leaps and rendering him insensitive to fatigue and pain.

20-21 *Following the customs of his ancestors, an Andean shaman offers coca leaves to the* apus, *the gods who live among the ice of the Cordillera.*

21 *Before his altar, a coastal shaman in Lambayeque uses divinatory and healing practices whose origins are lost in time.*

21

Traveling northwards from Lima we reach Chavín de Huántar, the ancient heart of Peru. It beat for nearly a thousand years, from 1200 B.C., and its religion and art spread to the great Pacific coast and through the Andes. Its grandiose monuments, dedicated to unknown gods with a jaguar's leer, reveal the existence of a theocratic state based on a religious concept which organized a huge workforce to exploit the scarce, miserly Andean soil and achieve specialization of labor, distribute products, and advance society. This work allowed the building of great temples and maintenance of priests who guaranteed the favor of the gods, revealed their will, and knew the times of the stars. It also allowed the digging of irrigation channels and production of food, especially maize, which fed men and gods with the sweet wine obtained from it, called chicha.

The divine figures with huge sharp fangs and terrible claws carved on the monoliths and stelas of Chavín signify that the order of the cosmos is based on the law of sacrifice, that death generates life and life generates death in a continuous cycle, and that the earth only gives fruit in exchange for the sweat of man's brow. Men nourish the gods with blood that turns into divine breath, and the gods nourish men with water, which is transformed into lymph and blood. In the basement of the Ancient Temple of Chavín a great knife-shaped monolith has been driven into the ground in the center of a sacred cross formed by underground corridors into which the sun penetrates on the day of the solstice, mystically fertilizing the earth.

Traveling upwards for another 50 miles or so we reach Huaraz, capital of the Ancash district, with its bracing 9,800-foot-high climate and cold nights. Continuing into Callejón de Huaylas, the magnificent panorama of the Andes unfolds. The huge steppes, at 13,000 feet, are green in the rainy season and golden in the dry season, resembling undulating seas, from which the flowers of Puya Raimondi, lady of the puna, rise up, tall and graceful. Above, lost in the blue sky, soars the permanently ice-capped peak of Huascarán (22,134 feet), father of all the mountains and supreme apu of all the Andean apus.

Riding up the mountain on horseback and being guided through this landscape, which seems to lead to the first morning of the world, is an experience that can revitalize your life, provided that you are empty of all thoughts other than the sensation of the cold wind, the warm sun on your skin, the magnificent distant snows, and the creaking harness.

After visiting the Paron Lagoon (15,798 feet) and contemplating the peaks and clouds reflected in its calm waters, you can ride down again and continue north, to the coast. The next stop is Trujillo, an ancient city of landowners and religious orders founded in 1534, its great Plaza de Armas shaded by slender palm trees.

Trujillo is situated in an area with a generous climate that produces fruit, cereals, and sugar cane. The first local organizations that claimed dignity and rights for the workers were founded in the Thirties in the latifundios of Trujillo and the great industrial sugar cane processing centers and strongly influenced the development of modern Peru.

In the vicinity of the industrial centers and the modern city stand some of the most famous monuments in the

Americas. Huaca del Sol, Huaca de la Luna, and the city of Chan Chan belonged to two cultures that existed in succession during the first millennium A.D.: the Moche and the Chimú. Huaca del Sol (huaca means "everything sacred") is a terraced pyramid made of air-dried bricks. It is 157 feet tall with a base measuring 748 feet by 446. According to tradition, this gigantic structure was built in only three days using 200,000 men.

In a square of the smaller Huaca de la Luna, recent excavations brought to light unmistakable traces of human sacrifice. Bodies, dismembered while still alive, were offered during one of the periodic floods that afflicted the Peruvian Coast, the first time to stop the rain, and the second to stop the drought, because the gods, or the chief god (the headhunter Ai Apaec, who had the fangs of a jaguar), had taken the request too literally.

Chan Chan was the capital of the fiefdom of the Chimú, skilled metallurgists who were deported en masse to Cuzco by the Incas to work for the sovereigns and gods. The huge silent ruins, to which the wind carries the smell of the sea, are surrounded by walls that are often over 30 feet tall and 13 feet thick at the base. There were squares designated for worship, temples that invariably had six niches

22 *The terrifying, three-thousand-year-old image of the jaguar god with his serpentine mane leers over Lanzón, the sacred monolith in the underground chambers of the ancient temple of Chavín de Huantar.*

23 top *The majestic temples of Chavín de Huantar (late second to early first millennium B.C.) prove the existence of a theocracy that was able to organize the work force around a religious idea, marking the transition to a high culture characterized by cities, irrigation canals, monumental temples, and large-scale cultivation of maize.*

23 bottom *The Portada, the entry to the main square of the Tschudi Citadel, one of the urban complexes of Chanchán (Trujillo), reveals the power of the lords of Chimú (eleventh-fifteenth centuries A.D.). Using anti-seismic devices, builders erected grandiose monuments of unfired clay bricks (adobes) mixed with cut straw, using seabird eggs as glue.*

dedicated to unknown gods in the walls, stores, and cisterns, and princely residences with thick walls decorated in relief with birds, fish, and geometrical patterns. It is pleasant to stroll through these sun-warmed labyrinths steeped in history, following the thin line of shadow cast by the walls and hearing the echo of your footsteps in the deserted squares.

Not far from Chan Chan stands the magnificent Huaca del Dragón, its clay walls overloaded with symbols including the rainbow serpent, lord of the rain. In the evening, the less squeamish visitors can visit the arena where cocks fight, fitted with deadly steel navajas attached to their spurs, in an iridescent whirl of wings, feathers, and blood. Others can watch the elegant dance of the marinera, who mimes a courtship with a Spanish flavor in which the suitor, wearing a straw sombrero and linen poncho, eventually overcomes the reluctance of a shy maiden dressed in long skirts and gaudily embroidered mantillas.

One hundred and twenty miles further north lies the sunny town of Chiclayo, surrounded by green expanses of sugar cane from which rum is distilled. At sunset, the fishermen return with the great red sun behind them, paddling their light reed boats (caballitos), while their womenfolk wait barefoot on the beach. They use the same boats as their ancestors, the Moche, used some 2,000 years ago.

Further north, amid fields of sugar cane over which loom arid rocky heights, stands Lambayeque. Legend has it that Naymlap, a king with a great headdress of bird's feathers, landed here from the sea with his bride and retinue. It is said that he knew how to fly, like the gods and witchdoctors. Naymlap built a temple where the emerald idol Yampallec, after whom the city is named, was worshipped. The Spaniards sought it in vain.

Lambayeque awoke from the torpor of the perennial tropical summer just over ten years ago, when tomb raiders followed by Peruvian archaeologists brought to light the ancient Moche priests and kings. They were buried at Sipán under the cotton and sugar cane, among the dusty mud huts with zinc roofs, at the foot of two huge red-clay pyramids. Their warriors, womenfolk, sentries, servants, llamas, and dogs were buried next to them, to guide them in the land of the dead.

There were also precious stones, silver, and gold; enough to fill room after room in museums and inspire treatises yet to be written. There was a collection of weapons, insignia, jewelry, figures, and liturgical instruments that reveal a sophisticated civilization, obsessed with religion and inebriated with the holy war that brought glory and supplied prisoners for sacrifice, not to the Sun as practiced by the Inca mountain people of the cold puna, but to the Moon, lady of the waters, nocturnal humidity, and lymph. This worship is understandable in an arid land scourged by the power of the daytime star.

From the plane, the pyramids, platforms, and artificial hills of Túcume, Batán Grande, Pampa Grande, and others can be seen emerging from the deserts and tilled fields. Their construction took centuries, and they survive as mute prayers, solidified in clay, begging the gods not to dry up the rivers that flow down from the Andes or to allow the earth to perish.

Outside the low houses scattered among the fields, along the roads, and in the sunny vegetable gardens are country people with faces from a bygone age. The same faces that the Moche molded in the portraits displayed in museums are revived by genetics, despite the passage of time and intermingling of races.

At night, Siec, the Moon, once the Lady of the Moche, rises slowly in all her glory beyond the blue hills, above the sugar cane plantations and pyramids, extinguishing the stars and making the waters of the river glisten. The moon is so large that it does not appear to be viewed from our planet. It can be admired in silence from a hilltop. This is an experience that floods the soul with light, despite the voracious mosquitoes.

Further north still, the sunbaked Piura, Talara, and Tumbes lie in deserts studded with green carob trees and thorn bushes. From Piura, after watching the famous caballos de paso (dancing horses) performing to the sound of Creole music, visitors can bathe in the warm waters of Paita or climb up to the sierra, towards Huancabamba, the traditional capital of magic and shamanism in Andean Peru. Traveling another 6,500 feet higher on horseback, the enchanted lakes of the Huaringas, where people bathe to leave behind sickness and misfortune, emerge.

During the journey you can see every variety of the local ecosystems, from the parched deserts of the coast to the arid cactus-studded steppes, from ceiba woods with their fat, green trunks to the fertile inter-Andean valleys crossed by clear streams and flocks of noisy iridescent parrots flying overhead.

After crossing the Andes, to the east we descend towards the Selva, the boundless stretch of trees that begins on the eastern slopes of the Andes and ends on the shores of the Atlantic Ocean. The largest rivers on earth run through the Selva, including the greatest of all, the Amazon, which originates at the confluence of the Ucayali (1,789 miles long) and the Marañón (1,110 miles long). Just before it joins the Ucayali at Puerto Franco, the River Marañón crosses the Campanquiz Mountain range, forming a narrow canyon only 197 feet wide and 1,641 feet long that runs between vertical green walls through which the waters of the river are channeled.

Before the canyon, called pongo de Manseriche, the Marañón

24 top *The great leaves of the gigantic Victoria Regia water lily float in pools in the Amazon rain forest.*

24-25 *An emeraldine boa, so called because of its color, sways wrapped around a cane. In the background is the Tambopata River, in the Madre de Dios region.*

measures between 2,300 and 2,600 feet from bank to bank. The water roars through the pongo, and the roar turns to thunder in the eternal iridescent mist. The Aguaruna Indians say that this roar is the voice of Cumpaham, the god who made the world and mankind, who lives hidden in the dark abysses of the pongo in the shape of a huge anaconda. When the canyon opens, the waters miraculously become still, there are flat, grassy banks to the left and right, and the sun illuminates the houses of Borja Village and the wide, tranquil reaches of the river.

Venturing off the beaten track in the Amazonian Selva, even for modest excursions, requires a spirit of adaptation and strong nerves in order to cope with the difficulties of the trails and the dangers that lie in wait, the insects, and temperatures that can reach over 100°F, with up to 100 percent humidity. The rains are frequent all year round, but they are especially heavy from January to June, reaching their peak in March and April when the rivers burst their banks and flood large portions of the countryside, turning it into swamps infested by hordes of mosquitoes, piranha fish, and leeches.

You cannot know the Selva if you merely visit the towns that stand on the river banks, great emporiums surrounded by labyrinths of foul-smelling canals that meander between tangles of houses on stilts, inhabited by Indians who are no longer Indians but not yet city-dwellers. Some of these towns, like Iquitos, still reveal traces of their turn-of-the-century splendor, when vegetable gold – rubber – was tapped in the Selva. To know the Selva you must at least board a motor boat and explore the minor tributaries, venturing into the interior, far away from the busy harbors. There, great curtains of lianas, blooming with orchids, hang like great festoons from the tallest trunks, entwined with gigantic branches among which monkeys play, hanging from dizzying heights and fraying into long green fringes in the sunlight.

The air is a warm breath that leaves the skin feeling damp. A thousand insects' wings fly through it, lighting iridescent sparks and leaving luminous trails in the sunbeams that filter between the leaves. The tree trunks are immersed in the semi-darkness of the undergrowth: giant ferns, thorn bushes, flowering shrubs, and bushes sprinkled with scarlet berries, plants with great leaves flecked with blood-red veins or black spots, and mysterious flowers. Moss and lichen thrive on fallen trunks that disintegrate into a yellow dust. On some stems the wings of great dragonflies gleam in the undergrowth, and in the shade, with its myriad of perfumes, birdcalls issue from the thick of the woods.

In the innermost areas, where the golden-eyed jaguar still roams and man does not venture, live the spirits of the wood, the "lords of the animals." Witchdoctors penetrate their kingdom through their dreams to make offerings and ask the spirits for permission to hunt their children: tapirs, large rodents, and the wary deer, which the men of the tribe hunt with the silent blowpipe or bow and arrow, only killing as many as they need to feed their families.

Caymans slumber and elegant flamingos stand in pools of shade and sun on the riverbanks, in the stagnant ponds, and on the hot sand. The last Indians of the Peruvian Amazon – the Aguaruna, Shipibo, Ashaninka, Campa, and Yagua, to name just the main ethnic groups, live in the midst

of the forest, along the minor tributaries of the great rivers. Only a few of them have kept their traditions, religion, and lifestyle more or less intact. The women grow a few species of vegetables – peanuts, sweet potatoes, and bitter cassava – in clearings made by their menfolk with axes and fire. The men fish, hunt, or exchange feathers, hides, herbs, and seeds with other groups of natives who act as intermediaries with the half-caste traders.

Unfortunately, the great Selva is dying; it cannot coexist with progress, which requires oil, gold, wood, land to raise animals, and open spaces for airports, roads, and towns. The Indians, once far more numerous than they are today, did not destroy the ecosystem because they were unacquainted with the concept of hoarding and believed that everything in nature has a soul.

26 top *Shipibo women wash clothes in the placid waters of the Yarinacocha Lagoon.*

26 bottom *Amazon natives still practice the custom of using blue* genipa *juice to paint geometric motifs on their faces. The type of design also serves to indicate their ethnic group.*

28-29 *Native women in the Chinchero market wear the characteristic hat and the* lliqlla *knotted at the chest, a traditional piece of woven cloth used to carry children on their backs.*

30-31 *The residential district of Machu Picchu is located in the eastern sector, along with the homes of priestesses, royal apartments, schools, and the tombs of nobles.*

Colombia

Ecuador

River Amazon

River Amazon

Iquitos •

Maynas

Tumbes •

Rio Marañón

Rio Ucayali

Piura •

Brazil

Sechura
Desert

Central Cordillera

Chiclayo •

Cordillera Oriental

Chanchán •
Trujillo •

Cordillera Blanca

Chimbote •

PACIFIC
OCEAN

Rio Urubamba

Huánuco •

Rio Madre de Dios

Huaylas •

Callao • **Lima**

• Huancayo

Madre
de
Dios •

Cordillera Oriental

Cordillera Occidental

Huancavelica •

Machu Picchu • • Pisac

Cuzco •

Peruvian
Plateau

Pisco •
Paracas • • Ica

Pucara •

• Nazca

Puno •

Bolivia

Lake Titicaca

• Arequipa

Chile

NORTH
AMERICA

ATLANTIC
OCEAN

SOUTH
AMERICA

PACIFIC
OCEAN

The Land of the Children of the Sun

32 top *Alpacas with their precious, soft wool graze in green meadows at an altitude of 13,000 feet, with the Vilcanota Cordillera in the background.*

32 bottom *The landscapes of Peru range from the sub-arctic climate of the highest Cordillera to the fiery nightmare of the coastal deserts. The waves of the Pacific crash against the bare cliffs of Punta Illescas in the Sechura Desert, one of the most arid in the world.*

33 *Descendants of the ancient Uru, extinct since the 1950's, wait for tourists where their ancestors once lived. Everything is as it once was: the islands made of totora, the houses, clothing styles, food, and language. Only their religion has changed, due to large-scale conversion to Protestant faiths brought from the United States.*

The Lake of the Fiery-eyed Puma

34-35 *The name Titicaca comes from the protective deity of the place, a puma* (titi) *with eyes of flame* (qaqa).

35 top *Colonial structures rise behind the lake on Taquile Island.*

35 bottom *Bright yellow totora stands out against the cobalt waters of the lake.*

36-37 *The shapes of Uru boats have remained unchanged over time.*

Peaks that are the Dwellings of the Gods

38-39 *In the province of Cuzco, little blue ponds fed by Andean snow are scattered at the feet of peaks over 16,000 feet high.*

39 top *Sharp rocky teeth and peaks covered with perennial glaciers in the Vilcanota Cordillera rise above the chilly steppes between Minaparayoq and Paqchanta.*

39 center *This stark panorama of rocks and snow is typical of the central Andes.*

39 bottom *Mosses, lichens, and wind are the only living things in the mountain area at the edge of the permanent ice in the Ancash district.*

40-41 *Sunset tinges the glaciers of Alpamayo (19,512 feet) with surreal hues in the Cordillera Blanca.*

41 *This magnificent image shows the frosty lace of the Santa Cruz Chico Glacier in the Kitaraqu Range of the Cordillera Blanca.*

42 top The *peak of gigantic Huascarán (22,134 feet) peeps out from behind wispy clouds, like a vision suspended in the sky.*

42 bottom *Every year, the glaciers of Huascarán claim a sacrifice of foreign lives. Native shepherds explain impassively that it is an offering for profanation exacted by the* apus, *or mountain spirits.*

43 *Suspended over fog-shrouded abysses and frozen steppes, the Chopicalqui Glacier (21,000 feet) rises over the Cordillera Blanca.*

44-45 *Taciturn guides accompany curious tourists on Andean ponies to the edge of the icy hell of Ausangate (20,916 feet) in the Vilcanota Cordillera.*

46-47 *The last light of day envelops Chinchey Massif (20,414 feet) in the Cordillera Blanca.*

Under the Sky at an Elevation of 13,000 Feet

48 top *Today as centuries ago, dry stone walls surround pens in Cañón del Colca, in the province of Arequipa.*

48 center *The huts of Sauranama* campesinos *emerge from the vast stretches of maize fields in Vilcashuamán, the "Land of the Sacred Falcon."*

48 bottom *A trail vanishes among the reeds on the shores of Lake Titicaca.*

48-49 *Her child on her back, a woman walks through the fields at Cañón del Colca.*

Fantasies of Nature

50 *Spires eroded by the wind stand out against the deep blue sky in the Rock Forest of Huayllay.*

50-51 *The latest giants threatened with extinction, the* Puya Raimondi, *enigmatic symbols of a vanishing world, rise over the Andean buttresses of Callejón de Huaylas.*

52-53 *Since Inca times, natives of Maras have used the hot, salty waters that gush out of the mountain.*

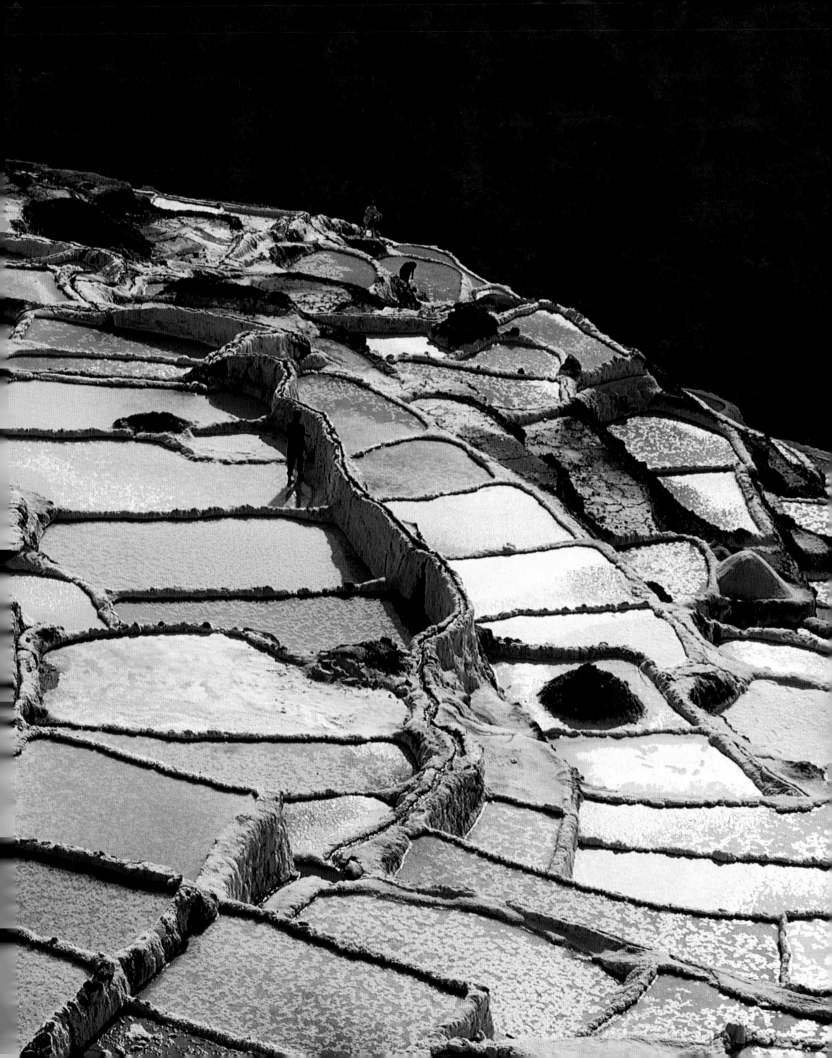

Where Desert and Sky Merge

54-55 *The bare cliffs and endless sand dunes of Paracas are home to unlikely fauna.*

55 top *Wading birds take flight in the Paracas Nature Reserve. Their white bodies and red wings inspired the colors of the Peruvian flag.*

55 center *Rocks carved by the sandy winds dot the desert coastline of Casma.*

55 bottom *A colony of sea lions populates the Paracas Nature Reserve.*

Amazonia: The Land of Green Mystery

56 *Lord of the jungle and the night, for millennia the jaguar (*Felis onca*), a divine beast, has been a symbol of the supreme deity and its creative and destructive capacity. Even today, it is the spirit animal that guides shamans along the paths of dreams.*

57 top *Immobile birds (*Phaetusa simplex*) lie in wait at the edges of the fish-filled marshes of the Amazon rain forest.*

57 center *Under the blazing sun, moist steam rises from the impenetrable maze of the Amazon jungle.*

57 bottom *The jungle rises like a green wall to the edges of the great rivers. This photo shows the Tambopata River.*

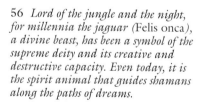

Cities for today and yesterday

58 top *Peru is a land of geographical contrasts and extreme social inequality, although this has diminished somewhat. Modern skyscrapers and pretentious buildings alternate with precarious dwellings overpopulated with families who struggle for daily survival.*

58 bottom *The white volcanic stone (sillar) of the Society of Jesus Church in Arequipa stands out against the background of a perennially blue sky. It is said that when Inca reached the fertile valley at the foot of Misti, he said to his generals, "Are, qipay!,"or "Good, let us stop," thus giving the city its name.*

59 *Where the Inca buildings of Cuzco (11,150 feet) once rose, today there are little Spanish-style houses along steep paved lanes.*

Lima: Spanish Memories and Avant-garde Architecture

60-61 *Due to Lima's urban expansion, the Government Palace, seat of the President of the Republic, is now almost on the outskirts of the city. Behind it rise the* barriadas, *the capital's most poverty-stricken districts.*

61 *The Puente Piedra crosses the river Rimac, once sacred to the oracles. Rimaq means "that which reveals destiny."*

62 top *The Archbishop's House (sixteenth century) was once the seat of the supreme religious power of an immense Spanish colony that included Peru, Ecuador, Bolivia, northern Chile, and a portion of Argentina.*

62 bottom *One of the most famous monuments in Lima from the colonial period is the palace of the Marquis of Torre Tagle, built in 1735.*

62-63 *The old library in the San Francisco Convent, founded in 1535 three years after the Spanish arrived in Peru, holds many precious texts, some of which have not yet been studied.*

64 top *The Park of Love, built along the Lima seaside promenade in the 1980's, reflects the old taste of the Spanish* azulejos *reinterpreted in a modern style.*

64 bottom *The Lima-La Oroya railway line leaves from the Ferrocarril Central Station in Lima, and runs along the highest-altitude train route in the world, the Ticlio Pass (15,982 feet).*

64-65 *The baroque façade of the seventeenth-century church of San Francisco is the work of the architect Constantino de Vasconcelos.*

66 top *Modern skyscrapers next to the old lighthouse testify to the urban development of Miraflores, one of Lima's most exclusive districts.*

66 bottom *North American-style bars and restaurants are designed to offer services primarily to tourists and affluent residents of Miraflores.*

67 *The central plaza in Miraflores is Lima's modern heart, poised for the future.*

68 *The rapid and uncontainable expansion of Lima, which began in the 1930s and accelerated over succeeding decades, has generated a number of smaller centers within the capital as a whole. One of these is Callao, which grew up around the port that, since the colonial age, had been the commercial heart of the country.*

69 *In the immense* barriadas, *the poor districts that squeeze the city like a vice, masses of the disinherited cling to a precarious existence. Over 15 years of terrorist war have caused two million* campesinos *to flee from the sierra, flowing hopelessly into the* barriadas *of Lima.*

Cuzco: The Navel of the Inca World

70 top *Improvised stands selling products from the sierra line the roads in Cuzco, the ancient capital of the Inca empire.*

70 center *The stone foundations of Inca palaces were preserved by the* conquistadores, *who built their dwellings on top of them.*

70 bottom *The Church of Santo Domingo in Cuzco stands on the Qoriqancha, or "Golden Fence," the most important temple dedicated to the Sun, ancestor of Inca kings. The walls were covered with sheets of gold and a splendid garden adorned the interior.*

70-71 *On one of Cuzco's secondary streets, an alpaca, Spanish-style houses, and a Coca-Cola sign denote the tormented path of history.*

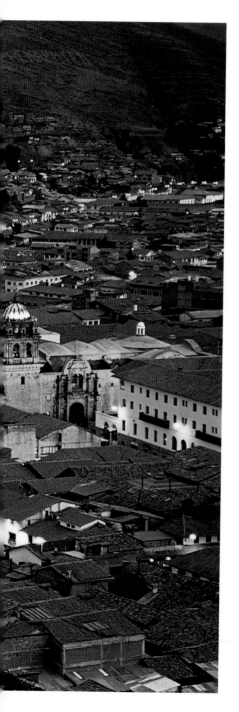

72 top *The hills where the fortified temple of Saqsayhuamán stands provide a panoramic view of the city of Cuzco.*

72-73 *Cuzco's central plaza stands on the ancient Waqaypata Square, where Inca and leading priests performed the most important rites. In the native tongue, qozqo means "navel," the spiritual and political center of the world.*

73 top *The main altar of the Cuzco Cathedral is covered with thick, embossed silver plate, just one of the things that make the interior of this church breathtakingly rich.*

73 bottom *Colonial religious architecture often reused the stones of destroyed ancient temples, as can be seen in the façade of the Church of Santo Domingo in Cuzco.*

Arequipa: The White City with its Great Volcanoes

74 left *The façade of the baroque church of the Society of Jesus in Arequipa is made of white sillar. The sumptuous decorations reflect the era when the powerful religious order was at its height of splendor.*

74 top right *One of the roads within the Santa Catalina city-monastery in Arequipa, which stands on five acres of land.*

74 bottom right *The cloister of the Society of Jesus is now the site of elegant shops selling typical regional items.*

75 *Continuing an ancient monastic tradition, a few nuns still walk through the porticoes of the Santa Catalina Convent, where the youngest daughters of Spanish potentates were once secluded.*

Iquitos: The Mestizo Heart of the Amazon

76 top *Colorful boats that ply the waters of the Amazon River by day are moored in the tranquil port of Iquitos for the night.*

76 bottom *The poorer houses in Iquitos, inhabited by* mestizos, *still reflect native construction styles.*

76-77 *Founded in 1864 on the banks of the Amazon River, the populous city of Iquitos experienced its height of splendor during the rubber fever that continued until 1910. Today it lives primarily on trade and tourism.*

Places of the Past

78 top *As exemplified in Pisaq, Inca architecture used local stone and was perfectly adapted to the environment. Respect for the balance between man and nature was and is still a fundamental feature of native religious thought.*

78 bottom *Walls of unfired brick protected the entry to the great architectural complex of Ollantaytambo.*

79 *The sacred city of Machu Picchu was buried under vegetation for almost 500 years. A few shepherds lived in part of it until it was "officially" discovered in 1911.*

City of clay

80 top *These unfired brick walls belong to one of the royal complexes of Chanchán, the Tschudi Citadel. The Chimú who built these monuments had a profound artistic sensibility. The wall decorations, depicting sea otters, are just one example.*

80 center *The Paramonga fortified temple, a colossal work of unfired brick, was built in the shape of a llama, a design that is recognizable only from above.*

80 bottom *The steps leading to the upper Paramonga Complex are made of slabs of stone as well as unfired bricks.*

80-81 *The monumental northern gate that leads to the main square of the Tschudi Citadel in Chanchán is decorated with typical stair-shaped Andean motifs. It symbolizes the three cosmic levels on which the priest-kings exercised their power: the world of the dead, the world of the living, and the world of the celestial gods.*

82 *The jaguar-like face of this Moche divinity from Huaca de la Luna, south of Trujillo, is reminiscent of archaic Greek representations of the Gorgon, but it actually depicts the terrible aspect of the supreme deity Ai-Apaec, creator and destroyer.*

83 top *The two-headed serpents that decorate Huaca del Dragón, also known as the rainbow serpents, are located just a few miles from Chanchán. They represent the rain god that the Incas called Amaru, the "Celestial Serpent."*

83 center *The leering Moche divinity appears with obsessive frequency in the art of this ancient people of the northern coast (second-seventh century B.C.), a reminder of the necessity of sacrifice, particularly human, in order to regenerate the power of the gods and thus nature.*

83 bottom *Recent excavations of ancient temples have uncovered colored wood sculptures like this one from the El Brujo archaeological site north of Trujllo.*

Archaeology and mystery

84-85 *The Inca site at Tambo Colorado is in the Pisco Valley. The largest tambos, like this one, located along major communication routes, were administrative centers, storehouses, and military quarters, with lodgings for travelers and stables for pack llamas.*

85 top *This geoglyph depicts a hummingbird. Perhaps the mysterious signs were emblems of the noble clans of Nazca society (i.e. clan of the hummingbird, clan of the pelican, etc.).*

85 bottom *Some of the Nazca lines mark the sun's point of exit on the solstice. Painstaking astronomical analyses have now refuted the theory that they are "stellar calendars."*

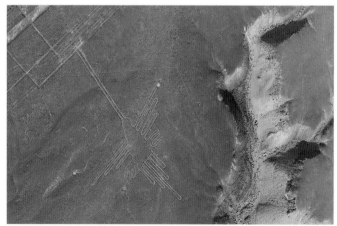

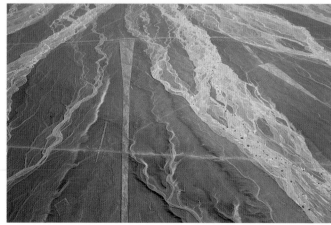

Machu Picchu:
Inca Peaks

86-87 *The citadel of Machu Picchu (7,218 feet) is comprised of two principal sectors separated by a square: to the west (left in the photo) is the religious core with the Temple of Three Windows, another religious edifice that may have been dedicated to Wiraqucha, the Intiwatana, and the Sun Temple; to the east is the residential area for clergy and perhaps Inca, schools for priests, and the tombs of nobles.*

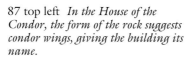

87 top left *In the House of the Condor, the form of the rock suggests condor wings, giving the building its name.*

87 top right *Dwellings were covered by roofs made of layers of straw (ichu). The sloping roofs ensured protection from torrential rains.*

87 bottom *The niches carved into the walls were used for pots, tools, idols, or lamps, depending on the use of the rooms.*

Inca Architecture

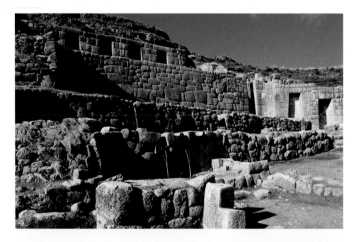

88 top *Clear water flows from the fountains of Tambomachay, a place dedicated to the cult of one of the manifestations of the Universal Mother: water. Machay means "cave," or perhaps it may refer to the great niches that symbolized access to the underworld.*

88 center *This door led to the architectural complex of Saqsayhuamán, the "Satiated Falcon." The architrave was put into place during recent times.*

88 bottom *In the chaotic period that followed the Spanish conquest of Cuzco and the attempted reconquest by Manco Inca (1536), Ollantaytambo was also used as a fortress. Nonetheless, the presence of temples, mausoleums, and purificatory fountains suggests that it was a religious as well as military site.*

88-89 *The magnificence of the cyclopic complex of Saqsayhuamán suggests the idea of a fortress. The plan of the ramparts, formed by parallel zigzags, nevertheless suggests a relationship with Illap'a ("The Thunderer"), an Andean god of lightning and thunder and bringer of rain. Construction dates back to Inca Pachakutiq (1438-1471).*

Where the Ancestors Stand Guard

90 top *The gigantic temple dedicated to Wiraqucha, the creator god, stands in Raqchi. Lodgings for priests and the sacred Aqllakuna virgins once stood next to the religious edifice, and were made of lava rock and unfired brick.*

90 center *The agricultural terraces (andenes) of Moray in the province of Cuzco, hug the contour of the terrain. The Incas used this solution to transform the Sacred Valley, traversed by Willkamayu, the "Sacred River" (today known as Urubamba), into a center for intensive agricultural production.*

90 bottom Chullpas, *individual or collective tombs, were probably built by the Colla people who settled in the Lake Titicaca region, although some experts still believe they were built by the Incas.*

90-91 *A burial tower* (chullpa) *in Sillustani. Chullpas of carved stone held the mummies of local chiefs.*

Pisaq: Partridge Mountain

92-93 *This glimpse of one of the residential districts in the Pisaq archaeological area clearly exemplifies the incomparable construction skills of the Incas.*

93 top *Perched below the rocky peak, the Pisaq religious complex is one of the most classic architectural works by the Incas.*

93 bottom *The Sun Temple is the heart of the sacred citadel of Pisaq. Inside, a rock is equipped with a gnomon (*intiwatana*) used for astronomical observations.*

Sipán: Treasure Saved from the Vultures

94 top left *Eroded by the weather, two pyramids watch over the ancient priest-kings of Sipán, who are buried in the platform across from them.*

94 center left *Hundreds of anthropomorphic pots were part of the burial trappings of the "Lord of Sipán."*

94 bottom left *The skeleton of the "Old Lord" (circa A.D. 150) is recomposed in a safe place.*

94 right Orejeras, *the ear ornaments of the kings of Sipán, were sumptuous objects, like this pair made of gold and turquoise, which belonged to the "Lord of Sipán" (circa A.D. 250).*

95 *On one of the* orejeras *of the "Lord of Sipán" we can see the figure of a Moche warrior chief wielding a club and a small shield.*

96 top *This feline divinity from the tomb of the "Old Lord" bears the emblem of the two-headed serpent on its head, a symbol of the rainbow and rain.*

96 bottom *The upper portion of the scepter-knife from the burial trappings of the "Lord of Sipán" shows the deceased as he prepares to sacrifice a prisoner of war.*

96-97 top *This gold sonajeras represents the supreme divinity Ai-Apaec with a sacrificial knife (tumi) in one hand and a severed head in the other.*

96-97 bottom *The scepter-knife of the "Lord of Sipán" is surmounted by a gold pyramid decorated with scenes of sacrifices. The silver hilt is adorned with war trophies.*

Faces of the Present

98 top *Dancers masked as Amazon warriors* (qhapa-chunchos) *take part in the Qoyllor Riti Festival in the Vilcanota Cordillera.*

98 bottom *The large, colorful Pisaq market, a very popular tourist attraction, offers typical products of the sierra: cabbage, potatoes, and carrots.*

99 *An unmarried woman in the Chinchero market wears a traditional costume, a conspicuous symbol of her cultural and ethnic heritage.*

Sierra People

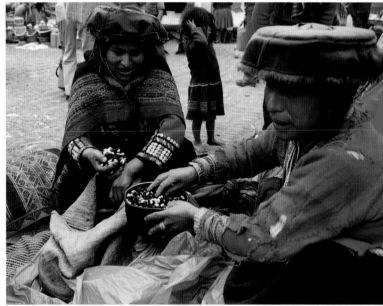

100 top left *At the Cuzco Station, a woman waits for the little train that runs to Aguas Calientes, a small town known for its hot springs and a departure point for excursions to the Machu Picchu archaeological site.*

100 bottom left *Typical dishes from the native cuisine are available at the Pisaq market.*

100-101 *On the ancient Inca Chinchero Plaza, women set up a market where they will sell local products to tourists.*

101 right *The Andean market is not only a place where products from various regions of the sierra are bought or bartered, but also a place for people from widely separated native communities to socialize and engage in cultural exchange.*

Native Features

102 left *This child will rest on his mother's back for a few more months. By the time he is five years old, he will begin to help her with domestic chores, and in all probability will continue to work for the rest of his life.*

102 top right *A mother with a child on her back, accompanied by a llama, is a common scene in Chinchero.*

102 bottom right *Village leaders* (varayoq) *go to church on Sunday holding the* vara, *a silver-decorated staff that is sign of their position within the community.*

103 *Like many natives of her age, this old woman from Chinchero may be wondering why the gringos take pictures of everything. It was once quite difficult to take pictures of old people, who believed their souls could be captured by a photo.*

The People of the Reed Islands

104 top left *The traditional houses of the Uru, on the shores of Lake Titicaca, now faithfully reconstructed for tourists, were once dwellings for lake fishermen.*

104 top right *This* totora *boat is the only suitable means of transport through the dense reeds of Lake Titicaca.*

104 bottom *A woman in the Uru islands cooks on a clay stove, which prevents the flames from spreading to the reed walls of her home.*

104-105 *Fishing was, and to some extent still is, the principal source of food for the people who live on the shores of Lake Titicaca.*

106-107 *The traditional reed boat is agile, light, and easy to manage, and can be maneuvered quickly.*

People at Work

108 top *The face of this child from Callejón de Huaylas, in the Ancash district, looks prematurely adult.*

108 bottom *In Pampa de Anta, grain is still hulled using ancient systems handed down over the generations.*

109 top *Potatoes are a typical product that originated in the sierra. Dried by lengthy exposure to cold and sun, they offer a nourishing food called* chuño.

109 bottom *Like all Andean mothers, this* campesina *from Huancayo works in the field with her child on her back.*

Interpreters of Mystery

110-111 *A diviner-healer* (curandero) *sprinkles offerings of perfume on his altar. In the foreground are rattles, the tip of a San Pedro mescaline cactus, and ancient skulls that hold spirit guides.*

111 *Shamanism in the Amazon Selva (based on plant magic) has its own rites, with a special vine known as* ayahuasca *used to reach a trance state.*

The Great Sun Festival

112 top *During Inti Raymi, the Sun Festival, there is a parade of ancient costumes from the four regions of Tawantinsuyu, the Inca empire.*

112 left center *The Inca opens Inti Raymi. In the background is the image of Inti P'unchau, the Shining Sun, lord of the world of men and father of the Incas.*

112 right center *A young* aqlla, *a "chosen virgin" dedicated to the cult, presents offerings of the Earth, including the maize that was used to prepare* chicha, *the fermented beverage used during rituals.*

112 bottom *Chosen virgins bring offerings of products from Pachamama, or Mother Earth.*

112-113 *The Inca invokes Taita Inti, Father Sun, while at his right the* Willaq Umu, *or supreme priest, raises the sacred pot of* chicha, *which he offers to the gods.*

The Raqchi
Festival

114 *This child from Sicuani wears the characteristic* chullo *on his head and a poncho hand-woven by his mother.*

115 top left *The weather-beaten face of this Indio participating in the Raqchi Festival in Sicuani reflects his exposure to wind and sun at an altitude of 13,000 feet.*

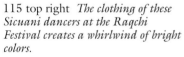

115 top right *The clothing of these Sicuani dancers at the Raqchi Festival creates a whirlwind of bright colors.*

115 bottom *The juxtaposition of old and new, like the dancers" traditional clothing combined with their shiny boots, makes Andean festivals quite fascinating.*

The Starry Snow Festival

116 top *The innate, ancient reverence of the native soul finds a Christian outlet in the Andean festival of Qoyllor Riti (Snow-Star) in the Vilcanota Cordillera.*

116 bottom *An offering of fire to the Qollqepunqu Glacier now takes the form of a lighted candle, but the intention has remained the same over the millennia: to ask Mother Earth for her fruits, the Sun for his light, the Sky for rain, and ancient and new divine powers for their protection.*

117 *Praying before the rock of the Virgin, used to venerate both Mary and the Earth Virgin who prepares her gifts for each new season within the depths of her womb.*

118-119 *Pilgrims from every part of the Cordillera come to the Grotto of the Virgin with lighted candles, a symbol of their faith. This sacred place connects the surface with the belly of the Mother Earth.*

The Dance of the Noble Warriors of the Selva

120-121 *Qhapa-Chunchos dancers wait to begin their performance.*

121 top *Ritual flagellation, a sign of penitence and a tool of purification, is an integral part of the Qoyllor Riti ceremonies.*

121 center *The Noble Warriors of the Selva (Qhapa-Chunchos) file past, accompanied by the sound of Andean instruments: the flute (qena) and drum (wankar).*

121 bottom *Characters in the Qhapa-Chunchos dance wear masks that resemble the feline leer of the ancient deities. Two serpents and a frog in the center are embroidered on the smock of the figure on the right, symbols of the fecund, life-generating Earth.*

The Silver Gate Glacier

122-123 *The Qoyllor Riti procession reaches the Qollqepunqu (Silver Gate) Glacier. The motifs carved in the candles represent stars in which, according to ancient tradition, the soul of every living being resides.*

123 top left *A Qhapa-Chuncho immersed in solitary prayer among the glaciers of Qollqepunqu.*

123 top center *An Ukuku dancer masked as a bear, a mountain spirit animal, sets his lighted candle in the ice. The candle is decorated with the ancient motif of the Andean stairway, a symbol of the cosmos.*

123 top right *The votive candles shine on the ice like tiny stars.*

123 bottom *Bear dancers (Ukuku) and savage dancers (Chunchos) bring the heavy, "dressed" cross up to the glacier at the end of the Qoyllor Riti Festival.*

People of the Great Rivers

124 top left *In the Amazon jungle, a forehead band is used to carry loads. Mothers use the same device to carry their children.*

124 top right *The young mother shown here belongs to the Campa del Gran Pajonal ethnic group.*

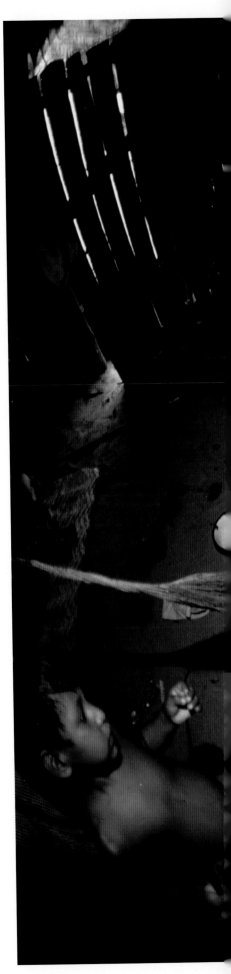

124 bottom *The hearth is lit in the hut, with a grate over the fire that makes it possible to smoke and preserve meat. Now metal containers have replaced the old clay dishware.*

124-125 *A family of Machiguenga Indios is immortalized in their hut. Due to the hot, humid climate, hammocks are better than any other type of bed or pallet.*

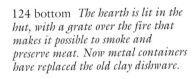

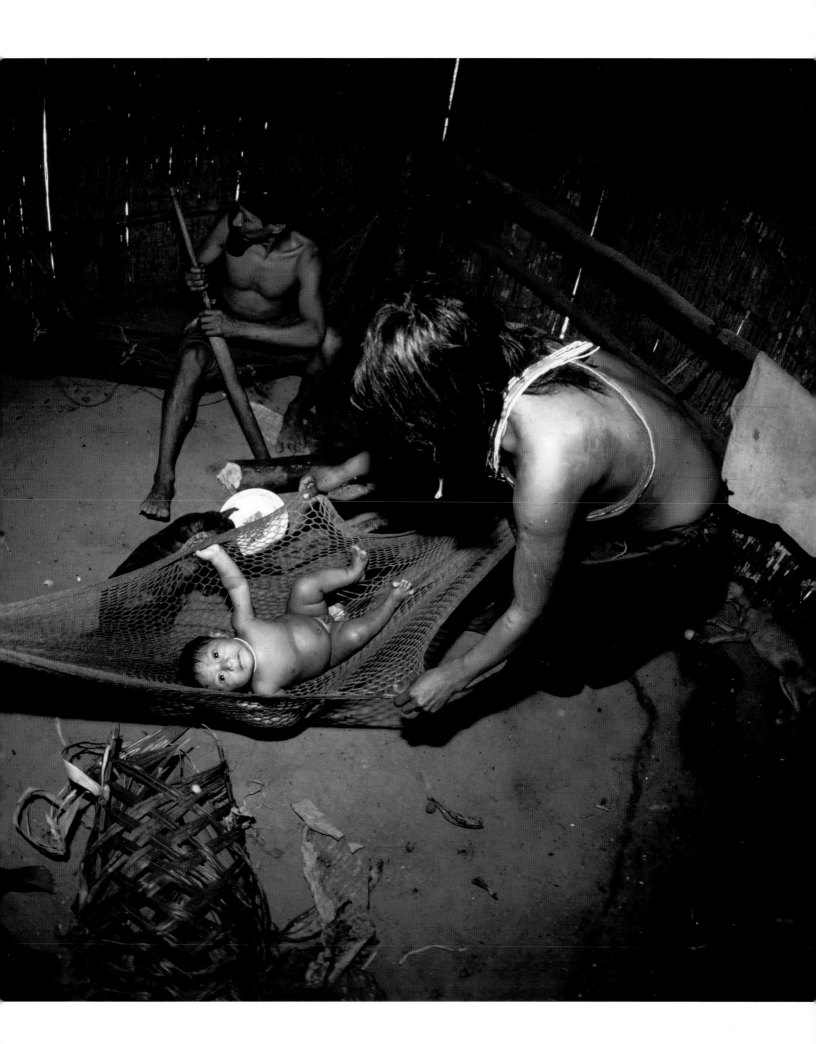

126 top left *A girl befriends a manatee in the Pacaya-Samira Nature Reserve.*

126 bottom left *Little by little, commercial clothing is beginning to replace traditional loincloths among the Indios, but the custom of transporting loads tied to the forehead continues.*

126-127 *An Indio prepares feathers for an arrow. His face is dyed red with* achiote *juice (Bixa orellana). His cotton tunic is typical of the Campa ethnic group.*

128 *Peru is a land of profound geographical, cultural, and social contrasts. It is a land where the past is still here and the present is slow to become the future. Perhaps this is the reason for its unique fascination.*

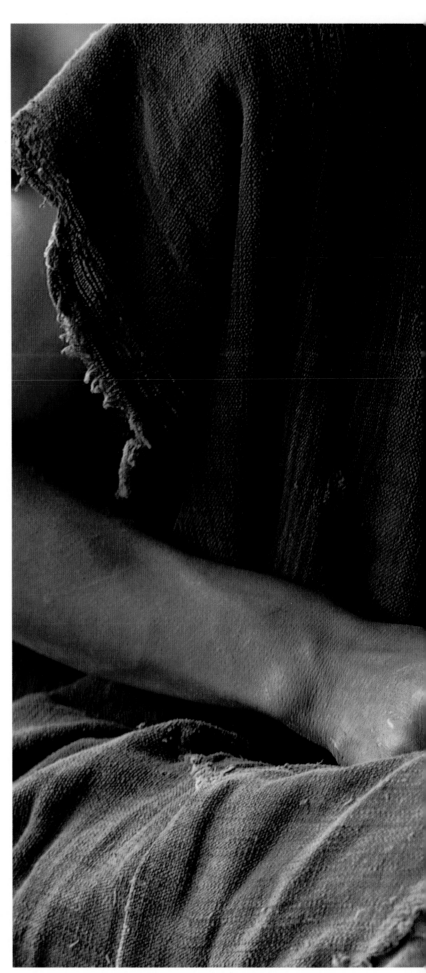